Hymns to the Beloved

A Call for Sacred Love

YOLA DUNNE

BALBOA
PRESS
A DIVISION OF HAY HOUSE

Copyright © 2011 Yola Dunne

All rights reserved. No part of this book may be used or reproduced by any means, graphic, electronic, or mechanical, including photocopying, recording, taping or by any information storage retrieval system without the written permission of the publisher except in the case of brief quotations embodied in critical articles and reviews.

Balboa Press books may be ordered through booksellers or by contacting:

Balboa Press
A Division of Hay House
1663 Liberty Drive
Bloomington, IN 47403
www.balboapress.com
1-(877) 407-4847

Because of the dynamic nature of the Internet, any web addresses or links contained in this book may have changed since publication and may no longer be valid. The views expressed in this work are solely those of the author and do not necessarily reflect the views of the publisher, and the publisher hereby disclaims any responsibility for them.

The author of this book does not dispense medical advice or prescribe the use of any technique as a form of treatment for physical, emotional, or medical problems without the advice of a physician, either directly or indirectly. The intent of the author is only to offer information of a general nature to help you in your quest for emotional and spiritual well-being. In the event you use any of the information in this book for yourself, which is your constitutional right, the author and the publisher assume no responsibility for your actions.

ISBN: 978-1-4525-3260-8 (sc)
ISBN: 978-1-4525-3261-5 (e)

Printed in the United States of America

Balboa Press rev. date: 3/3/2011

For Alain,

My partner in love

And for all who yearn

For mystical intimacy

"The minute I heard my first love story
I started looking for you, not knowing
How blind that was.
Lovers don't finally meet somewhere.
They're in each other all along"

Rumi

Contents

Introduction xi

Homage to my Beloved xiii

Poems 1

Acknowledgements 83

About the Author 85

Introduction

I am excited to share Hymns to the Beloved with you. The poems came to life because I asked myself a very important question; does a sacred and intimate relationship really exist?

I wondered if it was possible to bring forth into the world a relationship that reflects a divine union, attracting a soul mate that would wholeheartedly and soulfully unite with who I am. After years of failed attempts at having a fulfilling relationship, I had almost lost all hope that a deeper love was possible. Yet somehow, even through the ups and downs of love, I felt in my heart that my twin flame existed.

Then it dawned on me - I can write to him now as if he was alive. I can cultivate love inside me even if he has not yet manifested in my life. This is how the hymns were born; they are addressed to a lover I did not know with the goal that one day I would be reunited with my beloved in flesh.

One by one, the poems appeared. The words emerged gently in my consciousness as if they had a life of their own, and I recorded them diligently in a journal. Over the period of a few months I had gathered this collection of poems. I had no idea I would embark on such a deep spiritual journey of transformation.

Because the poems reflect such an individual journey, I thought it would be best to keep them secret and quiet. But then some friends became curious about what I was writing and I handed my journal over so they can have a peek – and I saw in their body language, especially on their face, how much they were moved by the words. To see their reaction touched me profoundly, and I learned a couple of essential lessons. Firstly, there is great value in sharing a profound personal story, because what is authentic for one person also resonates and belongs to all. Secondly, I realized the search for the mystical nature of love is an innate human yearning that exists, conscious or not, in everyone.

I want to share these poems with you because of the power, beauty and strength they have given me. I believe they are imbued with the vibration of love and can assist in opening the heart in an authentic way. In the simple desire to live a greater love, profound healing can take place because love is mystical and divine in its nature. By preparing a space for love, it finds its way home. It is attracted to its lover like a lonely stranger on a cold night walking into a warm home.

The poems feel like they carry a soft melody, like they have a rhythm of their own. I suggest that you read them slowly. Let the words help you find your own internal rhythm that will unlock the secret chamber of your heart. There is no wisdom in rushing this process.

Divine love has shown me a way to be more intimate with myself and with the soul of humanity. And then a miracle happened dressed in life's coincidences; I met the man of my dreams in a friend's garden on a beautiful spring day. And shortly after our meeting, the unique inspirational flow that helped me write the Hymns ended.

This book has now found its way to you. May it serve as a reminder that the path to sacred love is a journey worth taking and must be faced with courage, faith and stamina. I hope these poems will inspire you to keep going, to keep looking, to keep working at manifesting the intimate relationships that will serve your highest potential, and in return will be of better service to humanity.

Homage to my Beloved

My Beloved,
This is for you,
All of you.

I want you to know that I miss you. I have missed you for a very long time. I also want you to know how profoundly you have affected my life. In these pages I hope to honor the love I was born to express, the love that resides in the secret chamber of my heart.

I long for you. I feel your love in the songs of the world. Each day I make myself stronger so my love can reach you even deeper. In this sacred place of love, I am with you. I do not need to feed the illusion that I am alone.

The inner knowledge that you exist gives me hope and peace. I feel your respect and your touch. All I desire is to love you. All I desire is your happiness. You are such a tease, and such a gift. I desire more of you, more of us.

I believe in the power of our love. May this love find a way to bring us together. Wisdom tells me you will come soon. She says you are wise, true and real.

Until then, I am practicing my love for you. It is strong, loyal, and faithful. I feel you are alive, my love. My entire being tingles at the thought that we will be together soon. Let us cherish this dream together, and may sacred love make us whole.

My beloved,
When we are finally together in flesh,
I will cherish every moment.

Claim on Earth

Let us claim on earth
What is given in heaven
The veil of illusion
Is now lifted
Your love captures my soul
With loyalty and pure devotion
You are the fuel that lights my heart
You are my deepest passion
I pray to be graced
With faith, hope and charity
To make room for you
The garden is waiting
New love stirs
I am blessed
I feel you close
Reach for my hand
And capture my heart

Come Home

I ache and hunger for you
I want you close
In a blissful embrace
Adorned by devotion
And a deep humble love
I long for you
Come home my love
Come home now

The Desire of You

Thoughts of you tease me
Like sensual foreplay
My body trembles
With the hope of you
My lips wet with anticipation
For your brave surrender
You enhance me
Everything that I am
Shines brighter
With the desire of you

Love Reunited

You come to me in the dross of sleep
And I wake with a smile
With the scent of us in my memory
My soul longs to be with you
In the One Heart
Bodies intertwined
Like passionate snakes
Lost in each other's dreams

So wild we are
Our breathing heavy and powerful
Leading us together
To that blissful place
Love reunited
In heaven
I am the chalice
You, the Holy Spirit
On earth
You give me structure
I give you life
We are true mirrors
Humbly living
A divine secret
In joyful reverence
We know and celebrate
The secrets of life

In our embrace
We eradicate the notion of separation
Holy is the union
Of those who come together
In complete surrender

Unseen like a Dove

Soul on fire with the passion of you
You come to me in all waking moments
In between each breath
Unseen like a dove
Flying over a wintery terrain
Words come only in the language of hope
For you have been gone too long
From the conscious expression of my life
And now I wish you close
, Ever so close
Come warm yourself by the fire of my heart
Let me look into your eyes and discover
The meaning of life
Divine expression has conceived us
In its image we come together
Like drunk lovers swaying in ecstasy
At the reflection of the moon on water

Closer

The thought of you
Makes my body quiver
I have a longing
That can only be quenched by you
Like an endless source of pure delight
You are so close
And I want you nearer
Closer, yes closer
Come rest in my trembling arms
And let me lay my head
In the embrace of your love
Your words send waves of bliss
Into my body, my heart, my soul
We share the secrets
Only our love can tell
In this divine temple
Of bodies close
Silent
Bliss
Taking us further in the realm
Where lovers belong
I tremble again as you
Shake your way into ecstasy
Pouring your sweetness into me
Nourishing the power of my soul
Silent
Bliss
Love divine earthly made
In a sacred union full of us

Our Path

Let us come together now and boldly take a chance
To love, respect and know each other
To cherish each other's dreams
To trust our giving hearts
Living in complete devotion
To who we are

Let us risk the greatness
That awaits this courageous step
Toward each other
For we only have to surrender
To discover we have always been whole

Smile with me
For your happiness sends rays of hope
Deep within my heart
The love and union we seek
Is not an ordinary one
Many desire it
Yet few can give it
And even fewer can receive it

Let us make the extraordinary ordinary
Through the stamina of courage
Blessed by the transcendent power of goodness
The world may not know it possible
But a greater force wills us together
And cheers us on

Let us make this first step towards each other now
Trusting all is well
This is our path, beloved
And I am here with you
Hand in hand we will make it brighter, lovelier
Fulfilled by our common dream
That belongs to all

Abyss

I can see the abyss between us
And my heart responds with humility
In this moment my mind is clear
And finally I see not with my eyes
But with my heart, and the eyes of my soul

A Single Touch

A single touch by you
Makes me quiver
My breath quickens
My heart opens
Juices flow

You are filled with desire
For me, for us
I feel you pulsing
Harder with each heart beat
Coming into me like thunder

Your desire devours me
Like a wild beast
And I smile. I rejoice
I open up tenderly
Enticing you for more

Let us come together
Ever closer
Yes
Sweet surrender
Moments of pure bliss
Life reveals her mysteries

We are speechless
Breathless
Engaged in orgasmic thought
So precious
Yes

Love is never lost
I see that now
Love is never lost

Songbird

My heart sings
Even in the dead of winter
My heart sings like a songbird
Filled with spring

Love has shown me a path
I did not know
Offering clear sight through
The abyss of differences

Without you I am nothing
Without me you are nothing
Together we are everything
And so life sings

A song to find itself
Back into the embrace of goodness
Revealing the sacred nature
Of creation made true

Pulsing
Away
Into the Abyss

In
Out
Throughout

Pulsing
With Love
Taken by Thought

In
Out
Creation Unfolds

Pulsing
Me You
Yes

Anticipation

I feel you close
In the anticipation of us
My heart holds the memory
Of our union divine
You come to me tenderly
And I to you, wild
For finally I am here
In the place where I belong

Come close
Let us hold hands
Toward uncharted lands
Where only love reigns
Come close
Let us see
What mysteries lie within
Sighing we uphold our existence
Not knowing where one ends
Or the other begins

Love Builds Bridges

Let us give the best of what we have
And create a life filled with love
Delight, enchantment and beauty
Let us not wary too long in differences
Those that naturally take us apart

Love builds bridges, it does not destroy them

Make it Real

Let us find a way
To make love last
To make love grow
To make love burst our world open
With courage and stamina
Revealing that we can
Make it real, make it true

Already Understood

All is quiet
In this tender silence
I feel your touch near
The beating of my heart
Takes me deeper
In the silence
Of our embrace

Tender is your love
As it stands in the threshold
Of time and space
In this silence
I am safe
You take my hand
And I am whole

Some things forgotten
Are never lost
It's the knowing
We need to forget
In that empty space
Love finds us
And makes us new

In this calmness
Our souls meet
Beloved
No more wondering
How to know
For everything is
Already understood

The Door of Becoming

The smell of us
Permeates my imagination
I can still feel
Your sweat
Tickling my skin
Your lips
So tender
On mine
The rhythm of my heart
Still beats of us
Dreams of your tongue everywhere
And I lose my footing
In irrational thought
Here I find myself
At the door of becoming

Naked

In the strongest moment of my life
You have come to me
And made me weak
In the expanse of your passion
You devoured so much of me
I now stand naked
Empty
But this emptiness engulfs me
And gives new strength
Founded on the power of love
Giving
With complete freedom
Receiving
As if nothing was ever lost
In each other we find
The expression of life
That searches for itself
We love one another with courage
And become who we are

Sacred Lover

You captured my heart with the utmost humility
Opening a door that leads to sacred love
A part of me is afraid
I tremble like a shivering deer
In winter's cold embrace
The warmth you offer
Calls me to you
I am your lover
And you, beloved
Trigger my heart to expand
Beyond the limitations of mind
I still shiver in your presence
So long have I longed for your love
To gently warm my soul
In you I discover
The secrets of me
Only divine love
Can now ease my trembling
And so I fall to my knees
No words I can find to express
The divinity I have found in you
In our embrace
In our gentle surrender
To each other
For it is in this surrender
That all life is made conscious of itself
In this eternal beauty

True foundations are made
Vessels are built
To carry hope
In our hearts, and to the world
We are ordinary people
Living an extraordinary life
In the stamina of the soul
Comes the birth of a light so bright
It dissolves all fear
In the soft embrace of a humble heart
Oh sacred lover
Thank you

Love's Emptiness

Only silence
Knows how much I desire you
And love you
My wanting is akin to nothing else I know
It is what it is
You are the sacred fuel of my inspiration
You may know it not, but I do
Listen to the silence that brings us closer
No words can ever express
The alchemical reaction of my soul
In the presence of you
You have touched me once
And forever I am transformed
Listen with me in silence
May all words be lost
In the vast emptiness
Where love is to be found

Ray of a Tender Whisper

In the endless breeze
You softly whisper
My hearing
Becomes clearer
The wind
Takes us beyond
Imagining
Into
New life
Giving
Breathless
Receiving
Endless
Your voice entices
Joyful surrender
Into you
Us
Joy
The ray of a tender whisper

Beyond Doubt

I want you to feel
Beyond doubt
How much you are loved
I am always with you
Each moment of every day
Past, present, future
Nothing escapes
My love and devotion
For you, my beloved

I feel your trembling heart
Whisper to mine
You are never alone
My love is true
It is eternal
Blessing all that dare
To come near
Even for a moment
Of pure ecstasy

I am with you always
I have never left your side
Neither one can exist
Without the other
In deep humility
We embrace
Souls fly
Home

Beloved,
Still you elude me
It's okay. I'm not giving up
And neither are you

Space for Love

Blessed by original thought we are
Together as partners in the greatest dance ever known
Your tender love so bright
Illuminates joy
No more chaos can be seen
For all of life has engulfed itself in our embrace
Leaving space for love

~

The tenderness of love shows our true worth
The strength of love gives courage to overcome all obstacles
The flexibility of love discharges all judgment
The mystery of love keeps us humble
The power of love creates miracles
The gift of love transforms the self
Let us be still and know love

The World that Belongs to Us

Everything that I am is here
Everything that you are is here
Our worlds touch
With a tender kiss
Individually we are strong
Together, stronger still
Let us be soft, tender
Loving and kind
With this sacred merging
Let us stay strong and true
To who we are
And to each other
And lovingly create
The world that belongs to us

The Fire of Love

My heart pulses for you
So divine its expression
Looking into the abyss of love
Simply becoming more than I am
For you, for us
I am falling beloved
Deeper into the mystery
That makes us whole and unique
You take me in your embrace
Enticing me to be stronger
Bolder, lovelier
More of what I thought I was not
Becomes clearer
Some gains, some losses
All worth the transformation
In the fire of love

Destroyed by Love

You have taken me
I am speechless
Destroyed and devoid
Of all expectations
Separation is painful
As you know
Emptiness needs to be restored
For love to grow again
I wait for you
Dizzy from illusions
Gnawing at my mind
Like hungry birds
Even in this chaos I remember
Love brought us together
And this is never easy
The burning of two souls
For each other

Senses Transformed

I see more of you beloved
Ours is a great love story
Fueled by the passions of all
Who dare to go beyond restrictions
Set tightly in the world of fear

I feel you now beloved
Separation makes us stronger
When we reunite breathless
In the tender arms of recognition
All that we know becomes whole

I taste you sweet beloved
Engulfed in my senses as you surrender
To the trusting serpentine flow
Of our dancing souls
Dissolving differences into unity

I smell you close beloved
The essence of us permeates the air
In a human territory of pure delight
Where the divine is human, human divine
Joyful bliss takes me to eternity

I hear the sacred sounds beloved
Calling us closer
My voice carries you
As you bring yourself near
To see, smell, taste, feel and hear

Senses are transformed in loves embrace
Sometimes soft, sometimes strong
Together we dance the sacred dance
The morning remembers it still
And blesses the new day

I Want You

I want you
Broken and whole
Life makes us humble
Here we find strength
Here we find one another

I want you
Here I rest quietly
Trusting the sacred vision
Only my heart can see
The one our souls have made

I want you
Fulfillment true to itself
You are, I am
I am, you are
All of you becomes me, I, you

Warm

The sun comes in
And warms my face
It reminds me of us
Lost in an embrace
So tender and strong

The world turns
And I am untouched
By the distraction
That separates me
From you

Warm rays reach my heart now
I still find myself in fullness
The ecstatic freedom found
In love's surrender
I am made soft by your love

One Breath

I awoke in the night
To the sound of my breathing
Soon I discovered
It wasn't me making the sound
It was you my love
For that instant
Our breath
Became one
Blessings rushed through
For us, with us
Under the one breath
In the complete stillness
Our souls found each other
I was lucky to awake and witness
The true miracle of love
In the one breath

Be my Sun

Be my sun
The tender light
That nurtures my heart
Giving my dreams wings
Flying blissfully
In a world made true
By the courage of love

Softly whisper
The telling of your desire
So I may bathe
In the light of kindness
That frees the mind
Of erratic illusion
And restores hope

Dreams of Spring

I long for you
Like the seed dreams of spring
You are where I belong
The one breath
Reaches me everywhere
Imbued with desire
Adorned with pure bliss
Human, I am
In this discovery of love
That never ends
Only transformed
In the gentle embrace
Of goodness made true
I find myself again
And again
Longing for you

The Sea of Becoming

Take me sweet love
Like a ship's captain
To uncharted lands
Close your eyes, you say
This is a dream
Made real
By our love
Bliss takes me now
In your confident thrusting
Urging me forward, to stay true
On the sacred path of love
Bursting from the heart
Enchantment falls on us
Like a veil made of stars
We are lost now
In the sea of becoming

Elusive Love

In curious moments
You elude me
My heart quiet
From expectations
That normally take over my mind

In this quiet I surrender
What does not hold up to the divine light
Dissipates into the night
To be found again
In the birth of a new star

Far away you are
I listen for you
On the waves of time and space
Gentle pulse rising
Finding its way home
Quiet engulfs me
Together we stand
Before a vast ocean
Enticing us forward
Into the great mystery

Open the space between us is
Rejuvenating the heart
For what is real
True and everlasting
Souls meet, and with grace
They fall in love

~

Nothing can ever take away
The ecstatic moments
Between lovers
Life engorges with vitality
Passion knows
Its limitless freedom

Elusive love is always
Worth nurturing
For it will guide the brave souls
To the land of beauty
Adorned with blissful love
And the compassion of kings

Let love transform us
My beloved
Into the graceful creatures
Lovers truly are
Together we can dream again

Let me bathe in your passion
And you, in mine
The sacred fire
Brings our hearts together
In eternity

Desire to Love

Beloved, you consume my every thought

I long for you like my skin desires the gentle
spring breeze after a cold winter

My heart bursts at the thought of you, awakening my deepest passion

You are so elusive beloved

In the songs of the world I find you

Each breath taking me closer to the existence
that I know belongs to us

Patience escapes me as I do my best to hold
true to the passion in my heart

Yet something moves me

There is a stirring deep in my soul that
trembles with the desire to love

To let myself be consumed by the ecstatic perfume of love

In me, in you, we find one another

This is my deepest, most sincere of desires

The gentle return to a state of complete wholeness

This wholeness belongs to all living creatures

Let us adore each other, with the memory of the whole

Come to me my love
Surrender with me
In the abyss of time
Made into eternity
Take my hand
Walk with me
Into the unknown
Lined with the grace
Of miracles

Pulse Rising

I feel you pulsing inside me
You who has taken me
Bold in your desire
Focused in your loving intent
There is just one great pulse
Surrender we do
Together
Mind and body collide
Into the One Heart
Bliss
Ecstatic freedom
Unfolds in our tight bodily embrace
Come closer my love
Even closer
The moment has come
Silence falls
Rest
Until we hear the pulse
Rising again

Let us Fly

You inspire me beloved
To be more than what I can be
With you in my life
I can strive for new growth
Like a flower reaches for the sun
I am warmed by you beloved
You love me in such a way
That I am free to be who I am
For this, I am eternally grateful
Sometimes it is painful
Growth has a way of making things uncomfortable at times
Yet my heart is hopeful
That the love we share
The one that has called us together, is real
What a blessing this is beloved
I am grateful even when my heart trembles
Like the fluttering wings of a hummingbird
The strength I have in me is for you also
For so long I have searched for love
That is pure and strong and enchanted
Now I find myself in unfamiliar land
Where love takes me to you beloved
You stand so majestic
My heart fills with the overwhelming passion of love
And of life in recognition of itself
You, made earthly and human, are my deepest desire
Tears flow from a well of bliss

A fountain spurting out this truth
With beauty in its own song
I am who I am beloved
To be loved by you fully and authentically
Is the miracle that I seek
My life is a vessel
A true recipient of your love
Keep filling me beloved
I beg you, come to me
And never stop your endless flow and desire for me
I need it like the morning needs the sun to rise
Together we are made more whole, more real
The song of my heart tells me beautiful things
Its melody is tender and strong
Filled with a fiery passion for life
Sacred, mystical love is earned, beloved
May we be blessed by this grace
Come with me in true expression
I beg you, come with me
And hold my hand courageously
Grace will make it so
Love gives us wings
Let us fly

The Pain of Loving You

Sometimes the pain is so great
All I want is to become part of nature
Every molecule of my body becoming
Part of the grass, the trees, the rock
The water, the sky, the dark earth
I want to dissolve back into dust
To absorb the pain of loving you
Never have I thought of a love so great
Unimaginable until now
It surrounds me like a thawing spring fog
Each rain drop brings me back to you
I hear love call my name
Deep within me
Comes the song that will make me new
The pain of loving you
Stretches me across the landscape
Into the lands of unknown mystery

To Love You is Being Alive

My love for you pulls me closer to heaven
Closer to the realm where all possibilities lie
You inspire me, making each breath hurt
With the powerful presence of the divine
To love you is being alive
To love you brings forth the treasures within me
To come forth in the light of being
To love is all that I have become
Bursting in each direction of time and space
My heart finds you close
No matter where you are
No matter how far you hide
Don't hide beloved
My love finds you anyway
Loving you brings life closer to itself
And the world rejoices in this surrender

In your Eyes

Right now, you are all that exists
Love finds no other way but to express itself fully
In your eyes I see the mystery of life
And my heart flutters with anticipation
In your eyes I see meaning
I see hope in the way the rising sun
Shines on the dark earth
I find the freedom to fly
Supported by the wind
Weightless in mid-air
Unburdened by the thoughts that drag me down
Into the heaviness of suffering
In your eyes I am free
I hold true to who I am
You smile intently as you recognize
My surrender into you
Together we fly now
Free as life takes us
Into the arms of love once more

Sweet Touch

Come close
Hold me in your tender embrace
I am tired beloved
I am tired of not having you close
Love flows out of me
Like an endless fountain
Oh do I crave your love
Your sweet touch
A kiss so tender on my forehead
Uniting us in the peace
That all is well and perfect
Come close sweetheart
All that I want is you
Will you not come to me?
Yes that's it
Hold me close
Let me know your love
In this moment eternal
So I may know
Love is truth

My love for you
Takes me to my knees
Take everything from me
For I am no more

Sound of Silence

I am tired beloved
Tired of wishing you near
And only receiving glimpses
Of the greatness that can be

I see you looking at me
Curious, yet cautious
And this pains me beloved
For all I desire is your love

May the strength find me
To keep loving you
As I love myself
In the hope of you

I am tired beloved
Will you not give a sign
That the love I feel is real
And you want it as badly as I?

In the pure essence of who I am
I find you
This is my solace, my faith
That one day we will be together

Until then I cry beloved
Tears of pain and joy
You inspire me
Even in your absence

There is nothing I desire more
Than to love you, beloved
And to be loved by you
Like a sacred treasure

My heart breaks with the absence
I wish so feverishly to be quenched
By sacred love made human
Oh how I wish this to be real

I continue to move on
The forest path that is mine
You are always with me
If only in the sound of silence

The fire in my womb
Becomes greater, fiercer
I am tired beloved
Of fighting the absence of you

Rapture of Love

Love takes me in its rapture
My heart burns with the hope
Of the return of balance
A living goodness
In harmony with all life
The rapture takes me
Right in your arms
You extend your love to me
And decree that all is well
All is well and whole
In the rapture of love

Dervish Dance Part 1

Dance, dance, dance
You who are holy
Lead me to new heights
Only my soul can reach
Adorned in bliss
Extended in love
Lost in the sacred
Dissolved by the senses
Into one great dance

Dervish Dance Part 2

I am dizzy with your love
Nothing that I know makes sense
Broken open and naked I stand
At the tip of your outreaching fingers

I have a vision of you so close
The fabric of reality crumbles
Making me tremble intensely
In the magic current of love

Bird Wings

Beloved I am such a beginner at loving you
Yet my passion flows through my veins
Like an ancient memory
I am powerless in the expanse of this love
My heart belongs to you, and no one else
In the one breath we have found each other
Even in separation I feel you close like the blinding sun
At times you are darkness
I cannot find you, I cannot find myself
I hear the sound of my beating heart
And in this vast unknowing I find you once more
You belong to me, and I to you
I am a beginner at this love
Sometimes I am frightened
For only darkness surrounds me
In this invisible flame my soul burns
Each time I love, I burn
Then I am asked to love more
This flaming heart is eternal
It is a flame I can return to
Over and over again
I cannot bear to be away beloved
The pain is too strong
One cannot separate a bird's wings
Without killing it

Call for Love

Beloved
Let me experience
How much I am loved
All love given
Is never lost
Let me receive
The truth of love eternal

Heart Pounding

Heart pounding
Sweat pouring
I am called back to you
In the blaze of being
I am naked
With you closely entwined

Heart pounding
Sweat pouring
Life calls me closer
Mind blown to pieces
To be recovered
By sacred love

Heart pounding
Sweat pouring
Presence captures my soul
With the coolness of bliss
Rapture leads me
To you

Come Home

Deep passion is lit within me
I do not know how to contain it
My vibrating body wishes you near
It yearns for you in a way
Only love can embrace and make true
My thoughts are filled with you
I cannot bear us apart any longer
Come to me my dear
I beg you, come near
In the dancing flame I stand
Holding a vision true to the world
Creation knocks at my door
And speaks of you, of us
With the power of Grace I pray
That we are returned to each other
In the gentlest movement of my soul
My heart's path illuminates
Your way home to me my dear
Come home

Fountain of my Love

I am frightened
Dancing alone in the dark
I hear your heart beat
But you are not there
I cannot see you
Can my memory serve me now?
Does it suffice to make love grow?

I no longer wish to run
From the fountain of my love
It follows me anyway
Everywhere I go
Yet you are so elusive
Now it is my heart that sings
Of a tale old as the sea

Solace reaches me tenderly
In the quietness between thoughts
Remembering my origin
In its grand simplicity
Filling the darkness around me
With new hope
Of a world made true by our love

Living life without love
Is a fool's game
No longer am I willing
To belittle the desire of you
As if it matters not
To the spiritual starvation
Of a world engrossed in suffering

Your love gives me courage
Even when I see you not
My senses blind
Cannot take me away from you
And you, from me
The sacred dancer
Never loses her partner

Dancing Flame

All that remains from you
Is a small flame in my heart
It dances freely
I hold it dearly
A soft whisper can extinguish it
Just like a strong wind
Cannot touch it
This is the mystery of the flame
That lives in the sacred heart

You have come and gone
So many times now
In humility I stand naked
Not knowing what to make of it
I listen to the flame say
Love love love love love
I respond by smiling
For only a soul that has died
Can hear this song

In the Shadow

With pure devotion
I come to you beloved
Humility so great within me
I cannot help falling to my knees
No words can ever express
The love alive for you
For all of life has found me
In the shadow of you
And has taken me
Into your warm embrace

For so long I have waited for you
Now all I can find is silence

Life calls me back
With the voice of goodness

By looking for you
I found myself

The Heart Beats On

A lover never stops loving
Blessed are those who
Dazzle in her gaze
For even a moment of love
Given smiling freely
Can nourish the most lonesome
Lost in yesteryear

Alone the lover never is
Great light comes forth
Wisdom is the heart's protection
Discernment its ally
Humility its strength
Love its nourishment
And the heart beats on

You Are in All That I Love

Beloved
You have so many faces
Love is growing within me
Like the myriad rays
Of a thousand suns
You consume me
And as my flesh burns
My soul is born
Into an embrace so large
Yet easily contained
In a grain of sand
All light is to be found
In the seed of becoming
Beloved your love is grand
And I am so small
Yet you judge me not
You have found in me
A reason to be, to love
For without me, you are nothing
And I am empty, without you

You are in all that I love
The grass, a child's smile
A wise conversation
You bring me the light of the world
And with the mirror of my heart
I do my best to reflect it back to you
My sacred lover
My beloved
Let us keep this dance flowing
We are moved by the current of life
We are everywhere, you and I
My heart is content
You are in all that I love

Love's Residence

Even if I turn away from you
The flame in my heart
Does not subdue
You have made love's residence
Eternal and endless
Inside my sacred temple
That is you

Little Earth Angel

I saw you
In the face of a young girl
Telling me to be gentle
And patient
That it's really no big deal
Stop worrying and practice
Being who you are
Look at me she says
I've been practicing half my life
And look what I can do
My soul shines in you
Do not let it get tarnished
By your unwillingness to learn
If I can be patient with myself
So can you, she says
Her smile is radiant
Her small body flexible
Her will strong, her mind clear
Little earth angel I am
She says, and knows

Love is never lost
I see that now
Love is never lost

Faith Resurrected

In the silence
I hear your voice
My heart touched
Hears the melody
Of its song
Bursting with you
I am
Stay now beloved
Your form
Matters no more
Worries fade away
Faith resurrected
In your love
Your tender voice
Whispers all is well

Stay now beloved

Made Whole by Truth

You calm me
I cannot resist your warmth
What am I to you?
Can you feel my devotion
My loyalty, my love?
In you I have found
The tenderness to be who I am
Can you see the beauty of my soul
Made especially for you?
In the sacred mirror I look
I see the treasure that is me
Made whole by truth
Shining like a diamond
Hit by the light of a thousand suns
I am innocent once more
Like a worriless child
In the nurturing arms of endless love
All things created
Spring from our love

Worthy of Love

You show me
All life is sacred
There exists no hierarchy
In the circle of life
No one is ever left alone
In the power of love

Every single speck of life
Is worthy of love
Every tired heart
Deserves attention
With patient compassion
All is possible

Shattered Bones

I collapse in your presence
I am nothing now
But shattered bones
And broken flesh
My heart struggles
To stay alive
Blood everywhere
My soul elsewhere
Coming home

You are my Secret

I blush with you in mind
You are my secret
Dreams of you make me whole
Barely knowing you
Makes no difference
To the hope in my heart

Treasure Found

With each step taken
I find new possibility
In the expression of love
Grand is the mystery
That takes us further
Into the abyss of being

My heart races in harmony
Beating down the illusions
I am made to believe
Seeing more clearly now
I am exposed to faith
Who dresses me with hope

In the silent secret place
Where the treasure is found
You kneel before me
And offer your devotion
Our hands touch, like our hearts
We are made whole once more

Little Bird

Fly little bird
Fly
Into the heart of the beloved

~

Are you here yet?
I keep expecting you
You keep feeding me
Visions of you
Yet you remain
Elusive

~

Fly my soul
Like a little bird
On the wings of faith

Object of my Love

Inspire me
I have so much love to give
You teach me wisdom
Discerning the proper investment
Of who I am, in you

Compassion strikes
Thunderous and loud
Showing me that my longing
Is my ally
In loving you

The beauty of the world's song
Runs through me
Like a mountain stream
In awakening spring
Here is where I find you

The love I have for you
Belongs to the world also
Each smiling face before me
A mirror of my soul
Sparkling in the wind

Inspire me
I have so much love to give
Let my life be a vessel
Of my passion
In you I am

The object of my love
Comes and goes
Yet you remain
Devoted to me
In me you are

Only You can See

My body, strong, rested
Looks calm and tender
Only you can see
My soul on fire

I Expect You

I expect you
Your eyes
Brilliant smile
Saying
I love you

I expect you
Hand in mine
Heart closer
Wishing
I love you

I expect you
Mouth open
Mind intent
Looking
I love you

I expect you
Skin singing
Soft melody
Listening
I love you

I expect you
Body trembling
Lips wet
Glistening
I love you

Core of Life

I respond to you in silence
The quiet beauty of my heart
Leads me closer to the core of life
In this rhythm I find where I belong
I surrender to the endless search
The elusive truth of life eternal

Even in my Dreams

Even in my dreams
If I can give you hope
A glimpse of the beauty
That exists in all of life
I will have achieved much

Even in my dreams
If I can touch your heart
And you awaken
To the passion of who you are
My soul's thirst will be quenched

Look at Me

Let the longing be silent
Let it be quiet
It is never lost
Let it slip away
Into the bosom of the unknown
The invisible fire
Hotter than the sun
Will purify the soul
Dissolve into nothingness
Trust the power of love

Look at me
Look at me
I am never gone
You hear me?
Feel my love

Heart Ablaze

I had no idea
You'd come back to me
In such a way
Heart ablaze
Moments shared
In the light of the rising sun

Beyond

I bow beloved
In the sacred presence
Of our love
I am moved
Beyond speech
Beyond thought
Beyond mind
Into a place
Of humble becoming
In this reach
I find you
Waiting for me

Butterfly Wings

My heart is opening
And closing
Like butterfly wings
In my insecurities
Lies my strength
It is my soul now
Creating a sacred movement
Dancing with life I am
Even in stillness
All makes sense
In the opening and closing
Of a heart whose life
Is dowsed with passion
Beat on butterfly wings
Come and go as you please
I am with you
Neither here nor there
Flying free
In the great mystery
That is me

Gentle Footsteps

The rhythm of my heart
Beats like gentle footsteps
On the moist dark ground
My feet bare
Feel life pouring through
The kindness of love
Shatters my fear of being alone
Of being forgotten
I am the one who forgets
We are never apart my love
The love we share is grand
And is also contained
In the simplest deeds
The most invisible acts
Become visible
In the humble soul

The Living Universe

Love transforms me
Not knowing who I am
I belong as a child
To the living universe
Here I hear the song
We all long to sing

The Lion's Mouth

I have stopped looking for you
Heart beating like thunder
Courage takes me into the lion's mouth
Being devoured by my thoughts
I dare not move
I am still
Not out of fear
But out of love

Bonfire

Love is everywhere and in everyone
Who am I to judge, beloved
How it is intended to come to me?
Who am I to judge how my love
Given freely, affects the life of another?
Such is the mystery that belongs to love
And I am a lover, choosing a way of life
That holds the promise of life

I desire you all the time
Your mystical presence tickles my consciousness
Encouraging me to see the glory
Of the divine within me
Ours is not an ordinary relationship
It is quite extraordinary
It is alive and fiery
Quiet, still, intense and passionate

I do not know the meaning of patience
For so long I have craved you near
Above all else in the world I see our union as the most sacred
Being still in the presence of the bonfire of love
Is not an easy task; yet I am doing it
I am creating the space for our love to exist
Love manifests in a world where it is truly wanted

I find myself with you in the sacred place
Here we meet, in our full glory
To love each other, to embrace each other
Here we leave ordinary reality
And become the queen and king of our world
Around us is our kingdom
It is benevolent and made of goodness
Here we come to celebrate our love
We come to celebrate life
We come to forget who we are, dissolving in our embrace
Into a mystery that only the humble can come near

There is a great, deep silence
An emptiness so vast we become non-being
And slowly, the sound of life calls us back
We come happily soul to soul into our bodies once more

Each time we come together like this
We bring back a small piece of wisdom
Etched in the fabric of our relationship
This grain of wisdom light shines as it may
Delivering its gifts back to our kingdom, to each other
To our children, our families, to all that we love

And we love all, for love does not discriminate
We know this because we are living it
It is the fire that has found us by the grace of god
By the holy intention of goodness
We are blessed, my beloved
I never knew it was possible to love like this
Come and stay
Let us dance together now
And honor life's most sacred expression
Patient and still
I await your return

By looking for you,
I found myself.

Acknowledgements

Thank you Lina for being the first person to set eyes on this work. Your loving and generous feedback meant the world to me.

Thank you Cindi for your warm friendship and for providing such a cozy place at Café Les Saisons for me to write. My heartfelt thanks also extends to the patrons of the café who graciously let me have my favorite "spot" to write, and especially to Bruce for helping solve the problems of the universe while laughing so hard the ground almost shook.

Thank you fellow poets at One Stop Poetry, whose spirit of friendship and cooperation made me realize that sharing my poetry with others isn't that frightening after all.

Thank you Billy for shedding tears while reading one of these poems, and wishing to be alone and quiet with the words.

Thank you Spirit of Love for capturing my soul and making this work possible in the most curious and unexpected way. May you be my constant and loyal companion.

Thank you Rumi, Khalil Gibran, Caroline Myss, Marianne Williamson, Teresa of Avila, Andrew Harvey, Thomas Merton, Paul Ferrini and many others whose electrifying writings are a constant source of inspiration and make my heart sing with the joy of being alive.

Thank you Greg for the lovely conversations about love, relationships and the divine and also for helping me so often with the mysterious wonders of technology.

Thank you Alicia for your valuable help in editing this work. I cherish your friendship with all my heart. You are a true ally and soul sister.

Thank you my precious Jesse for teaching me that love knows no boundaries of time and space, and for making my heart so proud.

And thank you my beloved Alain, for believing in me and making my dream come true. You are my living miracle.

About the Author

Yola Dunne is a life and spiritual coach with myriad life experiences. Inspired by her passion for the divine and for human nature, she has been writing poems, essays and spiritual inspirations for over 25 years. This is her first book.

A lover of life, Yola enjoys growing her own food, writing, spending time in nature and sharing good French Canadian meals with family and friends. She lives in beautiful Chelsea, Québec. For more information about Yola, visit her website at www.yolaunlimited.com

www.ingramcontent.com/pod-product-compliance
Lightning Source LLC
Chambersburg PA
CBHW020016050426
42450CB00005B/491